Mo'olelo Pōkole

Learning Hawaiian Through Story

Moʻolelo Pōkole

Learning Hawaiian Through Story

Mya Hunter

GlossaHouse
Wilmore, KY
www.glossahouse.com

Moʻolelo Pōkole : Learning Hawaiian Through Story

© GlossaHouse, LLC, 2020

Requests for permission should be addressed in writing to the following:
GlossaHouse, LLC
110 Callis Circle
Wilmore, KY 40309
or at www.GlossaHouse.com.

Publisher's Cataloging-in-Publication Data

**Moʻolelo Pōkole : Learning Hawaiian Through Story.
Hawaiian.
Hunter, Mya.** Moʻolelo Pōkole : Learning Hawaiian Through Story / Mya Hunter. –Wilmore, KY : GlossaHouse, ©2020.

x, 84 pages ; 14 cm. -- (GlossaHouse modern language series)

ISBN-13: 978-1-63663-008-3 (paperback)

1.Hawaiian language--Textbooks for foreign speakers--English.
2.Hawaiian Language--Composition and exercises. I. Title. II. Series.

Library of Congress Control Number: 2020949062
Fonts used to create the front matter are available at
Linguistsoftware.com/ lgku.html

Text layout by T. Michael W. Halcomb
Typesetting by T. Michael W. Halcomb and Fredrick J. Long
Cover design by T. Michael W. Halcomb

*This book is dedicated to Loe, Loelani, and Kekaimalu—
For giving me this language. It is from your lives that I may
write these words. It is from your blood that I am Hawaiian.*

*And to my father, Jon, who holds no ounce of Hawaiian
ancestry, but has taught me everything I know about this land
and how to treat its people.*

*And to Michael Halcomb for believing in the writer within
myself and trusting in my story.*

*And to every politician and businessman who exploited our
land and water. The richness of these islands is in the people,
not your pockets.*

*And lastly, to my sweet Hawaiian Islands. You are the most
beautiful thing I have ever seen, and I pray this beauty isn't
fleeting.*

TABLE OF CONTENTS

GLOSSAHOUSE MODERN LANGUAGE SERIES

VOLUME 3

SERIES EDITOR

T. MICHAEL W. HALCOMB

GLOSSAHOUSE MODERN LANGUAGE SERIES

The goal of the GlossaHouse Modern Language Series is to facilitate the creation and publication of innovative, affordable, and accessible scholarly resources, whether print or digital, that advance learning and research in the areas of modern texts and languages.

Moʻolelo Pōkole

Moʻolelo pōkole: The Story of this Book
In these delicate inadequate words
I wanted to show you everything.
The things that I love,
where I came from,
who I was.
Follow
me.

Find me
folded between these words.
Beneath the stories of these pages I hide.
My culture spoke traditions,
passed down through peoples' lips.
Now I will write mine to last in peoples' hearts.
But in all these words do not look for me,
But find yourself.

This is the Genesis of Hawai'i Nei.
This is her birth story.
Genesis

Focal   Words: Ocean   (Moana: moh-ah-nah);   Volcano
(Luapele: loo-uh-pay-lay); Island (Mo-ku: moh-koo) Breadfruit
(Ulu: oo-loo); Bird (Ma-nu: mah-noo)

The **moana** (moh-ah-nah) had a different air about her. She
felt something small inside of her move and she smiled, for she
knew she would be a mother. Under her huge body, beneath the
depths of her water, where all light was squeezed out,
one **luapele** (loo-uh-pay-lay) after another, made up a small
colony of underwater volcanos that conversed in a harmony of
laughter. Their release of gas and bubbles rose to a crescendo
and fell in an undulating underwater symphony. As the ocean's
womb grew heavier, she began to prepare for the arrival of her
newborn. Finally, after thousands of years the agonizingly slow
crawl of the first luapele had surfaced. At its first taste of air, a
gasping release of smoke escaped its lips and yet, a wave
washed over it, submerging it beneath the cloak of blue. With
no witness, every day and every night, the pile of rocks breaking
through the blue abyss grew larger and larger.

Storms erupted over the moana, with clouds splitting open,
crashing down torrents of water upon the small achievement,
and burying it once more. The moana responded back in raging
fits of defiance, hurling ash from the luapele into the sky with
smoldering fury. Magma erupted from their mouths, steaming
at the touch of the cool sea. Year after year the moana labored
alone in slow agony to bring forth a chain of **moku** (mo-koo),
later known as the Hawaiian Islands.

When the moana had calmed her wailing child and the magma hardened, the rock that remained was black and porous, with sharp edges. Nothing fit for growing life. Corals began to form over the unforgiving rock, forming from the bodies of fish and grinded bones, to small sand pieces that smoothed the rock down. The sun set over the waters for many years before polyps emerged from the coral, which now bordered itself along the perimeter of the moku chain. The moana exhaled a sigh of relief, and rested from her delivery, seeing now that her work was done, and it was now up to life to get creative. A **manu** (mah-noo) flew from another distant place, and needing rest, landed on the rocky shores. Finding no food here, it emptied its bowels and took flight, almost as a thank you to the moku for providing a rest stop. Many other manu visited the new islands, as well as driftwood, harboring within its body, small bugs that had survived the perilous voyage.

Growing then subsiding, the islands methodically made way for life. Creeping plants broke from soil and slowly stretched to the sun. Manu would nest in their adult branches, and bugs would live in their stalks. The finest craftsmanship on earth took thousands of years to compete. And that craftsmanship is never truly done, for our islands are always changing, growing and adapting. The beguiling and enchanting islands, born of earths torments, were a raw, youthful, untouched emerald oasis. Ominous mountains that glowed red from dirt had ridged spines that made them look like coiled slumbering dragons. King palms grew on their backs and waterfalls slithered down their crevices like iridescent snakes. Caverns of crisp fresh water swelled in pristine crystal orbs beneath the breast of the land, waiting to be discovered. Tree branches hung low, bending towards the earth, with swollen **ulu** (oo-loo) dangling from their arms. Soft green ferns

3

grew in curling spirals and pollen dripped from the mouth of hibiscuses like honey. Luapele still remained active, and breaks scattered white sea foam on shores. Hot sand glistened in the young gold sun like millions of pearls. Wind funneled down from the mountains onto the land, shaking the grass and swaying the tress in a rhythmic ecstasy. And all this beauty remained untouched and unseen by man. The Hawaiian Islands sleepily laid under the clouds, waiting to be discovered.

Focal Words: Ocean (Moana: moh-ah-nah); Volcano (Luapele: loo-uh-pay-lay); Island (Mo-ku: moh-koo) Breadfruit (Ulu: oo-loo); Bird (Ma-nu: mah-noo)

4

PARTI

O'AHU

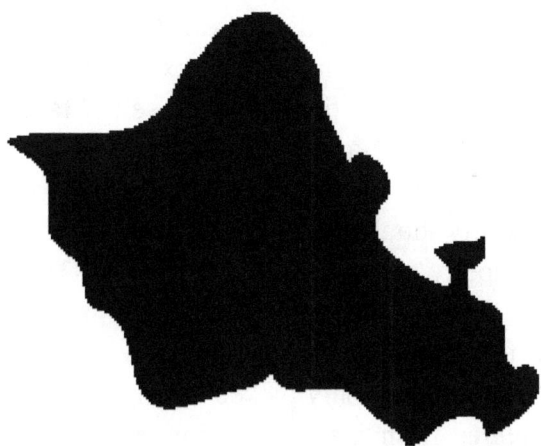

Ti Leaves

Focal words: Mother (Makuawahine: mah-koo-ah-wah-he-nay); Father (Makuakane: mah-koo-ah-kah-nay); Ahuimanu - A street name in the district of Kaneohe, which can literally mean "Flock of birds": (Ahuimanu: ah-hoo-ie-mah-new); Grandmother (Kapuna Wahine: kah-poo-nah-wah-he-nay)

Sundays are always dipped in the purest sentiment. The sun slipped her hands through the moisture that clung in the early morning heat. The mynah birds woke me up. Their chirping came from my window and their wings excitedly beat, causing soft thuds. "Pirate birds," I thought to myself. **Makuawahine** (mah-koo-ah-wah-he-nay) and **makuakane** (mah-koo-ah-kah-nay) had probably left for the market in the next town over. I slung a bag over my shoulder and ran outside. There was a gap between our property and the Methodist church. The chickens had become residents here. I briskly moved by the chained fence and ran to the end of the lot. Ti leafs bordered the open grass in a "U" shape. I only picked the dying ones because their color matures from green to yellow with brown spots. After I had filled my bag with ripened treasures, I drove to **Ahuimanu** (ah-hoo-ie-mah-new). I preferred the windows down in my car, and the wind rustled the leaves, shaking the water drops to roll onto the car seat.

"**Kapuna wahine** (kah-poo-nah-wah-he-nay)!?" I announced. I made sure to be loud so that she could hear me coming and not be startled. The hanging bell jingled as I opened the screen door. She sat in the back room watching Sunday golf on a pixelated box television. Her face, full of lines, smiled when she saw me, and I kissed her hello. We conversed, and I told her what had happened over the last week and how

6

the family was doing. I asked if she had gotten her mail that morning, and if she had eaten breakfast. She nodded. "I brought a surprise for you," I said. Turning around, I triumphantly held the bag of ti leafs I had picked that morning and placed them in her lap. Just as water knows where to move, we began to work.

It was not the type of work that is dreaded, but the type of work and company that I eagerly looked forward to every other sweet Sunday. The leaves were pressed, and steam slipped from the iron. I took scissors and carefully cut the spines out of the pile of warm crisp leaves. Th efingers of my kapuna wahine were curved from arthritis; nevertheless, she nimbly wove and braided. I was less graceful than her and held the base of the leaves between my toes and struggled to keep the leaves tight. Seeing this, my kapuna wahine laughed and told me, "You should never be afraid to restart, to create something that you love." And she helped me take leaves that were plagued with death and turn them into a halo of love—a ti leaf lei.

Focal words: Mother (Makuawahine: mah-koo-ah-wah-he-nay); Father (Makuakane: mah-koo-ah-kah-nay); Ahuimanu - A street name in the district of Kaneohe, which can literally mean "Flock of birds": (Ahuimanu: ah-hoo-ie-mah-new); Grandmother (Kapuna Wahine: kah-poo-nah-wah-he-nay)

7

Home

Focal Words: House (Hale: ha-lay); Family (Ohana: oh-ha-nah); Thank you (Mahalo: mah-ha-low)

My **hale** (ha-lay) is not confined to four walls, or a wooden structure. It sleeps amid humble oceans that reflect stardust filled skies and jungles that drip in emerald jewels of ferns and palms. My hale starts at the sand and stretches around the circumference of Oʻahu. Everything in between I call home. The people here are my **ohana** (oh-ha-nah) and the places are my sanctuary. Within their arms I find refuge and safety; yet, the skeleton of wood that I took my first steps in holds fast to my heart. I would like you to come in and take a look around. But before you enter please notice the sign on the front door that says, "**Mahalo** (mah-ha-lowh) for remov-ing your slippers." Downstairs is the guest bed and bath; you are welcome any time. The rattan couch creeks when people sit on it, but the hand stitched pillows will cradle your body comfortably. Up the staircase we display the Hawaiian flag proudly, above it hangs two parallel canoe paddles. Pictures of our childhood hang from the walls like ivy, and sun fills the windows like spring flowers. The kitchen cabinets are blonde wood. One of my favorite characteristics is the window above the sink that is lined with teacup-filled succulents, essential oils, and my mother's rings. Let me know if I can get you anything to drink. That relaxing smell is the diffuser that billows clouds of calming lavender. Atmosphere is important in a hale, and I wish for you to be comfortable here. The kitchen table was my Aunt Nalu's, and is very important to my Ohana. The circular koa wood table with matching chairs is where we commune in the mornings and give thanks in the evenings. Since there are no boundaries, plants grow just as wildly inside as they do outside. In case you already couldn't tell, my father likes orchids very much, especially the purple ones. On special occasions we eat on the outside picnic table on the balcony. And before you ask, yes, we keep Christmas lights strung outside here all year long. When the sun sets, our balcony offers an elevated view to make the sky look like melting oil over mountains. Mahalo for coming, you are welcome back any time.

Focal Words: House (Hale: ha-lay); Family (Ohana: oh-ha-nah); Thank you (Mahalo: mah-ha-low)

Sunday Markets

Focal Words: Kailua - A town on the east side on O'ahu (Kailua: kai-loo-ah); Fruit (Hua: hoo-ah); Leaves of the hala tree (Lauhala: lau-ha-la)

The car drove us to into the town of **Kailua** (kai-loo-ah). I fixed my eyes out the window and saw everything that was familiar to me; the drugstore, the fire station, the homeless man that always sits at that exact bus stop. Our Sunday routine was imprinted on my mind and it was my favorite day of the week. I grabbed all of our reusable bags and flipped through the crumpled bills in my hand. My eyes eagerly met stacks of piled bananas, fluffy heads of lettuce, and freckled papayas that were laid out on tables with smiling vendors who spoke to their customers like they were lifelong friends. *"How's the baby doing?"* ... *"How was the surf yesterday?"* This type of familiarity I took for granted as I ran past the bread and lychee stands to get in the line that had the "Fresh Coconuts" sign. I watched the man under the tent slice the top off the thick husk of the coconut with ease. The rough and shaggy remains fell at his feet. I look forward to this sweet treat every week. The coconut water slipped down the sides of my lips and I used the back of my hand to quickly clean up the fallout so that I could get to the soft meat as quickly as possible.

While I was only concerned with my taste buds, my mother used her hands to determine the good **hua** (hoo-ah) from the bad. She delicately picked up each mango to test its firmness and inspected its color. After she had finished shopping for the week's produce and talking story, we sat together to listen to the live music they always played. Men in **lauhala** (lau-ha-la) hats and sunglasses sang and strummed along that early

10

morning. Their bright smiles and tapping slippers were the true sign of local performance.

Focal Words: Kailua - A town on the east side on Oʻahu (Kailua: kai-loo-ah); Fruit (Hua: hoo-ah); Leaves of the hala tree (Lauhala: lau-ha-la)

11

Wahine of Hawai'i

Focal Words: Women (Wahine: wah-he-nay); Brown (Ehu: eh-who) Man (Kāne: kah-nay)

The **wahine** (wah-he-nay) in Hawai'i are the rarest in the world. Look at that one! The sun spreads on her tan skin like bronzed honey. **Ehu** (eh-who) hair slips to her waist in thick waves. Her eyes are like warm moons, the kind that you find at the end of the earth. Ripe like hibiscus, her flushed lips taste sweet and drip with nectar. Marks skim her hips from bearing your children. These scars are a sign of her sacrifice. When she sings, the flowers sway to her music as if she were the sun. When the gourd beats, she nimbly dances with fire at her feet, water at her hips, and wind in her hands. She steps lightly with generosity and grace, but raises her young like flowers in seasons of flood and drought so that they will grow stronger.

The wahine of Hawai'i are adorned with shells and gold around their necks and arms. They are draped in rich colors and simple fabrics. This is the wahine who was raised on an island paradise. She has the spirit of the restless ocean living inside her. She has ancestors who have been here longer then the trees.

The **kāne** (kah-nay) of Hawai'i will always have the reflection of curiosity and strength in his sunlight brown eyes. His beauty is best unkempt. His hair falls like the waves of the winter swell. See the sun baptize the skin across his arms and back when he paddles? The waves and salt refresh his heart and palms when he surfs.

Focal Words: Women (Wahine: wah-he-nay); Brown (Ehu: eh-who) Man (Kāne: kah-nay)

Da Bus

Focal Words: Work (Hana: hah-nah); Eyes (Maka: mah-kah); Baby (Pēpē: peh-peh)

I take the bus home from after **hana** (hah-nah). It's the time when the streetlights turn on to illuminate the night's face. I show the driver my pass and he waves me on. The bus rattles down the road with a voice intermittently crackling through the overhead speaker. Sand imbeds itself in the blue seat lining. I smile and think to myself, *"Only in Hawaii!"* I look around at the faces beside me. Tourists hold shopping bags in their laps, with cheeks flushed from the day's sun.

People in work uniforms carry tired **maka** (mah-kah) and some sleep with their possessions guarded on their lap like a dragon hoarding treasure. Men put their packs on the seats next to them and glance sideways at people through their thick rimmed glasses. They whisper back to each other like schoolboys. A mother holds her **pēpē** (peh-peh) on her chest with her purse in her lap. The uncle across from me thumbs a worn pack of cigarettes and continuously licks his lips.

People from all places commute here. From every part of the island comes a new story. Everyone is trying to go home to something, to someone. The driver stays silent. He takes time away from his family to make sure that people get home safely to theirs. Everyone who leaves tells him, "Mahalo." He nods in return and the doors squeak-close and he continues to the end of his route.

Focal Words: Work (Hana: hah-nah); Eyes (Maka: mah-kah); Baby (Pēpē: peh-peh)

Haben Girma

Focal Words: Young (Ōpio: oh-pee-oh); Help (Kokua: koh-koo-ah); Strong willed (Kamaehu: ka-mah-eh-who)

Hearing Haben Girma's speech about her life and being the first African American, deaf, blind, female graduate from Harvard Law School was utterly humbling. She has faced more adversity, prejudice, and obstacles in her life than most "seeing" and "hearing" people would ever image facing in theirs. She was not defined to what people told her she would be or what she would not achieve.

After her speech, the floor was open to a question-and-answer session. People lined up to type their questions on a keypad whose letters appeared on a brail board that Haben would feel with her fingers. Then, she would answer. When it was my turn, I walked onto the stage and sat down in front of the keypad. The lights beaming on the stage washed out every face in the audience.

I began to type, "Hello, my name is Mya and I have soooo many questions." As Haben read my comments out loud, the audience chuckled. I continued to type, "I am from Oʻahu, Hawaiʻi and language and culture is very important there. I am only beginning to learn about the language and culture of the deaf community. There are not as many resources for deaf kids on my island as there are on the mainland. As an **ōpio** (oh-pee-oh) woman, what can I do to **kokua** (koh-koo-ah) these kids?" She looked in my direction, paused for a moment, then said that when she was my age, the way that she made change was by contacting adults and people who held power to make those changes possible. I smiled and then typed, "Can I ask you a personal question?"

14

She answered hesitantly that it depended. The audience laughed again. I typed, "Is dating hard?" She paused again and then said that it was, but not just because she was deaf and blind, but that she is a busy woman who has a fast-paced job and a successful career.

I typed out that I was grateful for everything that she had taught me and how much she had given me through just one speech. I asked her if I could give her a word in Hawaiian. She nodded her head. I spelled out the word **kamaehu** (ka-mah-eh-who) and told her that it meant "strong-willed" and "determined." And I told her that she has lived this word throughout her life and that it was also the Hawaiian name that my parents had given me at birth. She smiled and reached her hand out to me. I shook her hand that felt so small in my own. This woman is incredible. An inspiration. A heroine.

Focal Words: Young (Ōpio: oh-pee-oh); Help (Kokua: koh-koo-ah); Strong willed (Kamaehu: ka-mah-eh-who)

Just a Girl and Her Chicken

Focal Words: Sun (La: lah); Clouds (Ao: ow); Chicken (Moa: moh-ah)

The hurricane was supposed to hit us that night. But, until then, everyone had the day to get water, board up their windows, and make sure their flashlights had working batteries. Every public school had been canceled so kids were more than thrilled to have a four-day weekend. I drove down the street and found that the roads were entirely empty. There was no **la** (lah), there was no wind, the earth seemed to stand still. I got my board out from my trunk, because with no cars and cool weather, the conditions for skateboarding were optimal. I sucked on the pit of a nectarine and slid a pack of soda crackers into the back pocket of my overalls. It was like I was carving down a deserted ghost town. Everyone's drapes were drawn, the **ao** (ow) seemed to be touching earth, and leaves crunched under my wheels. At the end of the street there was an old man sitting in a fold chair, like he was accepting the end of the world. I wondered how many times he had watched me go up and down that hill. I stopped to spit the seed out of my mouth and saw a **moa** (moh-ah). I pulled the crackers out of my pocket and, at the sound of the crumpling wrapper, she bobbed her head and waddled over to me. So, there I was before the hurricane, sitting in the middle of the road, just a girl and her chicken.

Focal Words: Sun (La: lah); Clouds (Ao: ow); Chicken (Moa: moh-ah)

White Cross on the Side of the Road

Focal Words: Ka'a'awa - A city on the far east side of O'ahu (Ka'a'awa: kah-ah-ah-vuh); Kane'ohe - A city on the east side of O'ahu (Kane'ohe: kah-nay-oh-hay); Heleconia - A tropical vibrant hanging plant (Heleconia: hel-leh-cone-yah)

A green Ford rumbled down the main road in **Ka'a'awa** (kah-ah-ah-vuh) headed back to **Kane'ohe** (kan-ei-oh-he) late one night. The headlights were a bright yellow glow, the radio was on, and the windows were rolled down so the driver could feel the warm Hawaiian night air. With one hand on the steering wheel, the other was slack, holding up a beer to the driver's lips. The road began to look narrower and the winding turns became more elusive and undefinable. The wheels of the truck danced across the white lane line. Lights from oncoming traffic seemed to get brighter and the driver squinted at the intensity and held up his forearm to shield his eyes and instinctively took a hard right, driving the truck into a telephone pole. Glass sprinkled the street and the driver's lap. The headlights of the car had gone out as well as the light in the driver's eyes. His head fell limp on the steering wheel, all life ventilated from his corpse. The next day, a white cross was perched in the ground at the sight of the crash. Flowers were hung, strung, and laid over broken glass, and around the cross. **Heleconia** (hel-leh-cone-yah) drooped from the white, outstretched arms of the cross. Notes from loved ones surrounded the space. This is a memory that too many in Hawai'i know and have grieved over.

Focal Words: Ka'a'awa - A city on the far east side of O'ahu (Ka'a'awa: kah-ah-ah-vuh); Kane'ohe - A city on the

17

east side of O'ahu (Kane'ohe: kah-nay-oh-hay); Heleconia - A
tropical vibrant hanging plant (Heleconia: hel-leh-cone-yah)

You Like Go Cruise?

Focal Words: Friends (Hoaloha: ho-ah-loh-ha); Sea (Kai: kuy); Sky (Wākea: wah-keh-ah)

My strongest memories of happiness and fun are when all my **hoaloha** (ho-ah-loh-ha) are together on a beach day. These memories are the ones that I yearn for and miss when I'm away or off-island, and the kind that I never want to end in the moment. I'll call up my hoaloha and ask, "You like go cruise after church?" Once we form a solid time to meet, we divide who brings the drinks, snacks, and tent. We love making trips up north. The beaches are wide, empty in the mornings. In the summer, the waves are flat and crystal clear-perfect for diving and fishing. And in the winter, the swell comes in and we play around in the monstrous shore break to get swept off our feet. When we arrive, we like to make our setup nice. We'll try our best not to get sand all over the blanket but, 30 minutes in, everyone's forgotten, and the blanket is coated. We pitch the tent and open the cooler. Ice cold aloha juice and coconut water are on standby for when it gets too hot. Someone sets up a speaker so we can jam all day long.

After the fishing poles are set up, we spend all day talking story, laughing to tears, swimming in the **kai** (kuy), and playing games in the sun. The **wākea** (wah-keh-ah) reflects the blue of the ocean. By the afternoon we are fried and beat. When everything is packed away, we'll go get Banzai Bowls. These are—no doubt!—the best acai bowls on the north shore. We all like to get different flavors from acai to pitaya with peanut butter, coconut, and bananas so that we can all try each other's. By this time, it's almost sunset and we go to a different beach to watch the sun wave goodbye beyond the horizon's back. The next day we'll probably have sunburns and find sand in our hair, but I wouldn't trade days like these for anything.

Focal Words: Friends (Hoaloha: ho-ah-loh-ha); Sea (Kai: kuy); Sky (Wākea: wah-keh-ah)

Duke's on Sunday

Focal Words: Waikiki - A resort area in Honolulu (Waikiki: why-kee-kee); Crowd (Lehulehu: leh-who-leh-who); Crazy (Lōlō: loh-loh)

Diamond head stands strongly in the background of **Waikiki** (why-kee-kee). The beach is a mix of locals and tourists who watch their children play in the calm shoreline. The time is about 3 in the afternoon and the sun is glazing my back when I start to wax my board. My leash is wrapped around my right foot and I get a running start into the water and begin the paddle out. When I reach the spot I want, I look back to the beach and see the rise of every beach umbrella and hotel. There's a **lehulehu** (leh-who-leh-who) of people forming at the entrance of Duke's restaurant. Duke's is such a popular and iconic spot, not only because it's named after a famous surfer, but because you can have free entertainment: watching the surfers while sipping a mai tai. It should be noted, too, that Henry Kapono plays this gig every Sunday afternoon at 4. People come from far and wide to hear him sing. He has a pretty loyal fan base and after they've had a couple drinks, that's when the dancing begins.

I catch my first wave of the day, the feeling is exhilarating. Surfing is hard work, but the feeling of standing up with the force of the water behind you is thrilling. As I lean to the right slightly to cause my board to turn, I see a turtle beside me. By the time the wave dies out, I lie back down on my board and begin to paddle out again. The water in Waikiki can be shallow; so, if you have to bail out on a wave, make sure to land flat or stay on your board so that you don't hit the reef.

After about 3 hours on the water I begin to paddle back in. My arms feel like noodles and my lips are salty. When I get out of the water, I can hear Henry playing. Perfect timing. I always like to paddle in on time to hear his singing at Duke's on Sunday. I begin to wash my board off in the shower and the sun continues to glow in the sky. The line for Duke's is out the door and the crowd dancing has a mix of interesting people wearing tutus to coconut bras. Upon seeing this, I laugh. When the song ends, Henry tells everyone that he'll be back to play next Sunday. I hoist my board over my head and commence the walk down the strip back to my car.

Waikiki is filled with all sorts of people and at night the **lōlō** (loh-loh) ones like to come out. They (mostly) won't bother you. On my walk back, there are street musicians, artists, a man with 5 parrots on his arms, and a man yelling and kicking at a bush. Drunk people stumble home and other surfers dash over crosswalks. I wonder what Waikiki will look like in 50 years? There has been so much development here that the pictures from 40 years ago compared to now make my heart sink a little.

Focal Words: Waikiki - A resort area in Honolulu (Waikiki: why-kee-kee); Crowd (Lehulehu: leh-who-leh-who); Crazy (Lōlō: loh-loh)

Part I: Vocabulary Review

- Ahuimanu - A street name in the district of Kaneohe, which can literally mean "Flock of birds" (Ahuimanu: ah-hoo-ie-mah-new)
- Baby (Pēpē: peh-peh)
- Bird (Manu: mah-noo)
- Breadfruit (Ulu: oo-loo)
- Brown (Ehu: eh-who)
- Chicken (Moa: moh-ah)
- Crowd (Lehulehu: leh-who-leh-who) Crazy (Lōlō: loh-loh)
- Eyes (Maka: mah-kah)
- Family (Ohana: oh-ha-nah)
- Father (Makuakane: mah-koo-ah-kah-nay)
- Friends (Hoaloha: ho-ah-loh-ha)
- Fruit (Hua: hoo-ah)
- Grandmother (Kapuna Wahine: kah-poo-nah-wah-he-nay)
- Heleconia - A tropical vibrant hanging plant (Heleconia: hel-leh-cone-yah)
- Help (Kokua: koh-koo-ah)
- House (Hale: ha-lay)
- Island (Moku: moh-koo)
- Ka'a'awa - A city on the far east side of O'ahu (Ka'a'awa: kah-ah-ah-vuh)
- Kailua - A town on the east side on O'ahu (Kailua: kai-loo-ah)
- Kane'ohe - A city on the east side of O'ahu (Kane'ohe: kah-nay-oh-hay)
- Leaves of the hala tree (Lauhala: lau-ha-la)

23

- Man (Kāne: kah-nay)
- Mother (Makuawahine: mah-koo-ah-wah-he-nay)
- Ocean (Moana: moh-ah-nah)
- Sea (Kai: kuy)
- Sky (Wākea: wah-keh-ah)
- Strong willed (Kamaehu: ka-mah-eh-who)
- Sun (La: lah) Clouds (Ao: ow)
- Thank you (Mahalo: mah-ha-low)
- Volcano (Luapele: loo-uh-pay-lay)
- Waikiki - A resort area in Honolulu (Waikiki: why-kee-kee)
- Women (Wahine: wah-he-nay)
- Work (Hana: hah-nah)
- Young (Ōpio: oh-pee-oh)

MOLOKA'I

Uncle Lemana

Focal Words: Fishpond (Loko'ia: loco-ee-ah); Sing (Mele: meh-lay); Loincloth (Malo: mah-low); Rock (pōhaku: poh-ha-koo); Spiritual energy of power and strength (Mana: muh-nuh)

My church group drove an hour from our camp to do some restoration at a local **loko'ia** (loco-ee-ah) on the island on Moloka'i. The drive there was on one straight road and not a single streetlight or sign was to be seen. Small houses occasionally popped out from behind tall grasses and abandoned cars. The mountains looked different than the ones on my island; these were jagged and dark like hands outstretched to the heavens.

The vans pulled up to the loko'ia. We hopped out and the hot sand met our calloused feet. The kids formed a circle around the entrance and began to **mele** (meh-lay) in order to ask permission to enter the space. Uncle Lemana and his sons who lived at this loko'ia received our mele and welcomed us. The kids around the circle giggled when they saw Uncle, and their eyes darted from him to the sand. Uncle Lemana was tan. He was so tan it looked like he was made of bronze. He had a woven palm visor and long white whiskers that sprouted from his round chin. His kind eyes had crow's feet tan lines from squinting. But what most people were laughing at was the fact that his attire consisted of a mere **malo** (mah-low) and black rubber boots. The malo was a bright red cloth that seemed stressed against the weight of his stomach that almost shaded the malo completely. The scary part was when he would turn around or when the wind would blow.

We found ourselves waist deep in the loko'ia searching for **pōhaku** (poh-ha-koo) beneath the clouded waters. I grasped a pōhaku and pulled it out of the sand and water so that I could throw it upon the top of the crescent shaped wall that formed the loko'ia. We were trying to repair the parts of the wall that had gotten knocked over or eroded by the waves.

At the end of the day, we returned to the shore exhausted and with some scrapes. We all communed together on the sand to mele and then eat. I sat next to one of his sons who taught me how to make a palm visor. I was grateful for this new knowledge he had given me and returned the favor by teaching him how to fold a cross out of the left-over leaves. I looked around the circle of people and saw tired sunburnt faces and disheveled hair. Some kids were even picking sand out of their lunches. That made me smile.

We packed up all our stuff and formed a circle to pray over the land and preform one last mele. Just as we were about to drive away, his son came running out to the road and was calling my name. I stuck my head out the window and he grabbed my hand and looked me in the eyes. It was a most wild look. He said, "We shared **mana** (muh-nuh) today." And then he quickly pulled away and ran back. I sat back down in the van and knew exactly what he meant. I had felt it, too, and understood that it was very special and rare. I think about this experience often and feel blessed to have shared and experienced his mana.

Focal Words: Fishpond (Loko'ia: loco-ee-ah); Sing (Mele: meh-lay); Loincloth (Malo: mah-low); Rock (pōhaku: poh-ha-koo); Spiritual energy of power and strength (Mana: muh-nuh)

Hapa

Focal Words: Half (Hapa: hah-pah); Chief (Ali'i: ah-lee-ee); Goddess of fire and volcanoes (Pele: peh-lay)

I can hear it
> The pounding of the gourd
>> on windswept sand.

I can feel it
> The pull of the mana
>> back to my birth land.

The **Ali'i** (ah-lee-ee) take one look at me and say:
> Her skin has lost its color.
>> Our flowers won't grow on skin that isn't as
> rich as dirt.
> Her voice is higher pitched.
>> How will she sing our chants as deeply as the
> ocean?
> Her feet and hands have grown soft.
>> She is no longer fit to walk upon the rocks
> formed by **Pele's** (Pele: peh-lay) fire.

You have
> lost our breath.

I have
> become an alien;
>> A stranger to my nation;
>> A foreigner in my own land.
>> An outcast.

The people in my new land ask me what I am.
I don't know.

Their mouths
      can't form my name.
Their minds
      can't wrap around my race.
Their hands
      don't fit around my neck.

I do not fit
      in their box.
I do not belong
      in their world

I am estranged.
I am strange.

I am straddled
          across an ocean
    Divided
        by blood
    Cursed
        by two tongues

Was I born
      of man?
      Or,
Was I borne
      by land?

Focal Words: Half (Hapa: hah-pah); Chief (Ali'i: ah-lee-ee);
Goddess of fire and volcanoes (Pele: peh-lay)

Coconut Grove of my Heart

Focal Words: Finished (Pau: pow); Harmony (Lokahi: low-kah-he); Broken (Poloke: poh-loh-keh)

We spent the day amidst the shore of Moloka'i, tucked away in a rotting wetland. The black trees dropped decaying coconuts into mud infested with venomous, plump centipedes, writhing worms, and creeping wolf spiders. The thick waters were murky and filled with black sludge. The land was plagued with a shadow of death. The wetlands made it impossible for machinery to come in; so, all the work had to be done by hand.

But this piece of land to me was more than just a laborious task. It was more than just work that wouldn't be **pau** (pow) for weeks. This vile, stench land was my heart. Rotting, and full of decay. However, cleaning out this wetland would be much easier than upending the internal onslaught of the darkness in my heart. Why? Because I had let things grow, fester, pool, rot, and decay for years. And I would've continued to let them, if God had not had a different plan for me. But it is beyond painful to remove things that have been there, grown there, and been loved, things that you thought were beautiful but, once in daylight, are vile. But although I saw the ugly, I refused to remove it. And I never would've touched it, if God had not had a different plan for me. He restores **lokahi** (low-kah-he) in the most barren of lands and in the most **poloke** (poh-loh-keh) of hearts.

Focal Words: Coconuts (Nui: noo-ee); Finished (Pau: pow); Harmony (Lokahi: low-kah-he); Broken (Poloke: poh-loh-keh)

Return

Focal Words: Elders (Kapuna: kah-poo-nah); Children (Keiki: kay-kee); Blue (Polū: po-loo)

I return to our traditions of gathering, taking my place next to Kekaimalu. The baby in her arms plucks at her face, and she leans over to devour him in kisses. Looking up from the table, I can see the faces of my **kapuna** (kah-poo-nah) and the **keiki** (kay-kee)—those who have come before me and those who will come after.

I return to the glances of warm **polū** (po-loo) waters. These are my father's eyes.

I return to the feeling of salt sticking to my skin like Velcro, and the hands of the bronzing sun. The plumeria flower whispers softly against my cheek and her scent drips thick.

I return to Moloka'i.

Focal Words: Elders (Kapuna: kah-poo-nah); Children (Keiki: kay-kee); Blue (Polū: po-loo)

Pink

Focal Words: Morning (Kakahiaka: kah-kah-he-akah); Colors (Waiho'olu'u: vai-ho-oh-loo-oo); Night (Pō: po)

Like fresh toes, ten in count
in the **kakahiaka** (kah-kah-he-akah),
Dawn's shy appearance
swaddles over rosy clouds.

Like blood's flush on first kiss
in the evening,
Dusk glows when she spreads
her limbs
over the horizon's back.

At the end, our **waiho'olu'u** (vai-ho-oh-loo-oo) fade.

In the **pō** (po),
the crackling of the sun
wanders into Night's web.

Focal Words: Morning (Kakahiaka: kah-kah-he-akah); Colors (Waiho'olu'u: vai-ho-oh-loo-oo); Night (Pō: po)

Catch and Release

Focal Words: A type of ray-finned fish found in tropical waters (Mahi Mahi: mah-he-mah-he); Boat (Moku: mo-koo); Fish on (Hanapa'a: ha-nah-pah-ah)

As the sun lowered in the sky, she began to slap the oceans back with her glistening glitter. We ran to the end of the pier road and casted ourselves into the water. We must've looked like a crazed school of **mahi mahi** (mah-he-mah-he) chasing after fish with all of the flopping, kicking, and splashing that we were doing. We pulled our soaking bodies up onto the floating wooden dock like fisherman hoisting in their catch to the **moku** (mo-koo). "**Hanapa'a** (ha-nah-pah-ah), hanapa'a!" we yelled as we reeled one another up onto the dock with our imaginary fishing poles. Until the last sliver of sun disappeared, we flipped, pushed, and flopped off the dock like catch and release.

Focal Words: A type of ray-finned fish found in tropical waters (Mahi Mahi: mah-he-mah-he); Boat (Moku: mo-koo); Fish on (Hanapa'a: ha-nah-pah-ah)

Starlight

Focal Words: Until we meet again (A hui ho: ah-who-ee-hoh); Black ('Ele'ele: eh-lay-eh-lay); Holes (Puka: poo-kah); Star (Hoku: ho-koo)

We said **a hui ho** (ah-who-ee-hoh) to the daylight. Sitting on the cool sand, I could see the light pollution from the next island over. The sky was **'ele'ele** (eh-lay-eh-lay) where we were, and without even a streetlight in the day, the dark was able to roam free during the night. It clung low to the island and hunkered down upon us. The only light that we were able to distinguish was the piercing **puka** (poo-kah) in the night's back that revealed **hoku** (ho-koo) clusters that blessed us with their jeweling brilliance.

Focal Words: Until we meet again (A hui ho: ah-who-ee-hoh); Black ('Ele'ele: eh-lay-eh-lay); Holes (Puka: poo-kah); Star (Hoku: ho-koo)

It's Everywhere

Focal Words: Sand (One: oh-ney); Hair (Lauoho: lau-oh-ho); Beach (Kahakai: ka-ha-kai)

The **one** (oh-ney) crunched between my toes and embedded itself in my clothes, it entangled and stuck in my **lauoho** (lau-oh-ho). It sprinkled along my cheeks and in the outer corners of my eyes. One is everywhere. It is always here. It's in the seats of my car and on the benches in the bus. It trails into grocery stores and falls out of my shoes. We take a part of the **kahakai** (ka-ha-kai) everywhere we go. I wonder if the one is different in Moloka'i—another place of paradise, another tropical sea spot that is naturally beautiful.

Focal Words: Sand (One: oh-ney); Hair (Lauoho: lau-oh-ho); Beach (Kahakai: ka-ha-kai)

Part II: Vocabulary Review

- A type of ray-finned fish found in tropical waters (Mahi Mahi: mah-he-mah-he)
- Beach (Kahakai: ka-ha-kai)
- Black ('Ele'ele: eh-lay-eh-lay)
- Blue (Polū: po-loo)
- Boat (Moku: mo-koo)
- Broken (Poloke: poh-loh-keh)
- Chief (Ali'i: ah-lee-ee)
- Children (Keiki: kay-kee)
- Colors (Waiho'olu'u: vai-ho-oh-loo-oo)
- Elders (Kapuna: kah-poo-nah)
- Finished (Pau: pow)
- Fish on (Hanapa'a: ha-nah-pah-ah)
- Fishpond (Loko'ia: loco-ee-ah)
- Goddess of fire and volcanoes (Pele: peh-lay)
- Hair (Lauoho: lau-oh-ho)
- Half (Hapa: hah-pah)
- Harmony (Lokahi: low-kah-he)
- Holes (Puka: poo-kah)
- Loincloth (Malo: mah-low)
- Morning (Kakahiaka: kah-kah-he-akah)
- Night (Pō: po)
- Rock (pōhaku: poh-ha-koo)
- Sand (One: oh-ney)
- Sing (Mele: meh-lay)
- Spiritual energy of power and strength (Mana: muh-nuh)
- Star (Hoku: ho-koo)
- Until we meet again (A hui ho: ah-who-ee-hoh)

BIG ISLAND

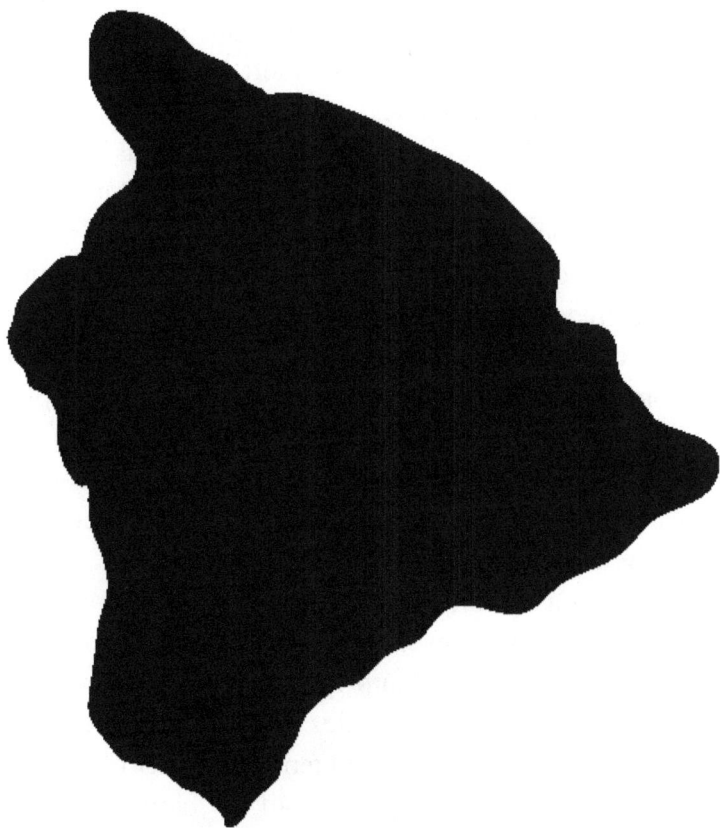

Jungle Symphony

Focal Words: Rain (Ua: oo-ah); Thunder (Kahekili: kah-ha-key-lee); Wind (Makani: mah-kuh-knee)

Two sliver vans full of children spiraled up the top of a hill that connected into paths for hiking trails. The vehicles parked beneath the thick trees and unloaded. Out poured wearisome teenagers through the sliding doors. I left my shoes in the car so that I could feel every dry leaf under my feet and all the dirt around my toes. The crew embarks on a mysterious hike that no one had been on and whose length was unknown. My curiosity, like a magnet, pulled me to the front. Deep into our trek, I felt the **ua** (oo-ah) on my hair. I looked up through the canopies of leaves and green and saw the clouds grow dark. Most of the kids complained and turned back. They did not want to get wet by the incoming showers. The ua fell harder and soon enough a jungle symphony commenced. The drops splashed on leaves and the wild orchestra became deafening. My excitement ran wild. I and one other boy stayed on the path and slipped through the mud. We slid in the ua laughing the entire way.

I was having so much fun losing myself to the walls of the woods that, when we paused to look behind us, the only traces of humanity were our own footprints. We watched them quickly fill with rain and form into puddles. My body shivered and my hair stuck to my back in drenched tendrils. Water ran down my nose and into my mouth; it soaked all my clothes through. It was a wonderful feeling. It was like a baptism, a sort of being born again in God's creation. Every raindrop that fell off me was like stress or fear making. I started feel lighter and more alive. I paused to celebrate, to dance, and spun through the slimy mud with my arms outstretched like I was imitating the trees around me. The jungle symphony of the ua only became louder and I only danced harder until I had to search for breath. In my heart, I thanked the earth for this blessing to the land. The ones who turned back forget that this land's water runs through their veins, and that this land's water has magic that can heal their blind eyes and hearts.

The clouds that showered water now crackled with the foreshadowing sound of **kahekili** (kah-ha-key-lee). The low rumble of the sky's drum sent my heart and feet racing faster. The ua became blinding and stung from the force of the **makani** (mah-kuh-knee). And as much as I wanted to be a part of this world, I knew that I would never be as quick as the makani, as strong as the ua, or as strong as the kahekili.

Focal Words: Rain (Ua: oo-ah); Thunder (Kahekili: kah-ha-key-lee); Wind (Makani: mah-kuh-knee)

Not Your Average Sand

Focal Words: Feet (Wāwae: vah-vai); Voyage (Huaka'i: who-ah-kah-ee); Battles (Kaua: kah-oo-ah)

>Ashes beneath my wāwae (vah-vai).
>Cigarette powder underfoot.
>Grounded up shadows and
>Secrets of each wave.
>
>Each lap.
>Each grasp upon shore.
>
>I wonder who walked here before me?
>   This beach keeps every footprint.
>
>I wonder who will come here after me?

Were **kaua** (kah-oo-ah) fought on these very shores?

Were ships launched to **huaka'i** (who-ah-kah-ee)?

>Black sand specks my skin like soot.
>I look out into the water and spot
>a small riptide forming.
>This is a black sand beach on
>The Big Island.

The sand here feels different beneath my wāwae. This matcha-colored sand is powder and pebbles underfoot. It's like the earth met the ocean and decided to make this beach an emerald rarity. The green sand beaches here are a must-see, too.

Focal Words: Feet (Wāwae: vah-vai); Voyage (Huaka'i: who-ah-kah-ee); Battles (Kaua: kah-oo-ah)

It Takes a Village

Focal Words: Hands (Lima: lee-muh); Eyes (Maka: mah-kah); Mouth (Waha: vah-ha); Heart (Pu'uwai: poo-oo-vai)

It takes a village to form the foundations of our lives.

It takes a village to make you the woman that you have become.

Faces of the kapuna stand behind me with their blessing.

We are all holding hands from beginning to the end.

Did your **lima** (lee-muh) have to dig in the red dirt of earth's skin so that mine may raise up in a fist?

Did your **maka** (mah-kah) have to bear the sweat of labor against you brown so that mine could watch mountains fall?

Did your **waha (vah-ha)** have to carry the wind's chants so that mine could cry out in protest?

Did your **pu'uwai** (poo-oo-vai) have to beat in the labor of our land while mine beats to keep that land alive?

If only you could see what they have done…what I am trying to do.

It takes a village to protect what you have built for us.

It took a village to make who I am today.

And it will take a village to make you.

Focal Words: Hands (Lima: lee-muh); Eyes (Maka: mah-kah); Mouth (Waha: vah-ha); Heart (Pu'uwai: poo-oo-vai)

The Name Game

Focal Words: Bless (Pōmaika'i: poh-my-kah-ee), Peaceful Ocean (Kekaimalu: ke-kai-mah-loo), Strong Willed (Kamaehu: kah-mah-eh-hoo)

A parent doesn't get much say in what their baby will look like. That's up to genetics and, well, God's design. A parent does, however, have control of how their child is raised, and this can affect the child's behavior in negative or positive ways. But does a parent have control over their child's personality? In Hawaiian tradition, the name that you give your child is what they will become. That might sound confusing but, traditionally, the Hawaiian name that you are given is what you are meant to embody and influence your personality—who you are. Hawaiian parents use this as an opportunity to **pōmaika'i** (poh-my-kah-ee) their children with certain attributes.

When my sister and I were born, my parents took a lot of time and thoughtful consideration when giving us our Hawaiian names. My sister was born first. My parents gave her the Hawaiian name **Kekaimalu** (ke-kai-mah-loo). This means "Peaceful Ocean." When I was born, my parents gave me the name **Kamaehu** (kah-mah-eh-hoo). This means "Strong-willed" or "Determined." Our whole lives, my sister and I have carried these attributes which were given to us by our parents. Parents have an opportunity to speak life into their children. How? By giving them a word, a single word, that they will carry for the rest of their lives.

Focal Words: Bless (Pōmaika'i: poh-my-kah-ee), Peaceful Ocean (Kekaimalu: ke-kai-mah-loo), Strong Willed (Kamaehu: kah-mah-eh-hoo)

Dreams from Southern Shores

Focal Words: Pueo (A short-eared owl that is endemic to
Hawaii: poo-eh-o); Green ('ōma'oma'o: o-mah-o-mah-o)

I dreamt upon a **pueo** (poo-eh-o) wing, a sacred feather.
The **'ōma'oma'o** (o-mah-o-mah-o) marsh waters
churned it back and forth,
Taking their time to craft with sands from southern shores.

I hope it flies into your mind and remains tethered.
Balance upon your countenance, earth's greatest treasure.

Those jasmine eyes steady upon the sanded shores
They never waiver or stray but remain fixed as jade.
Those jasmine lips meeting mine with a feathers pressure.
The moon murmurs her songs of eternity to our ears.

The feather's luck among these cat-tailed reeds has spent.
In the marsh, the herring shines beneath the slippery waters.

The pueo watches between the twisted branches,
His feathers floating among the sky's starlit descent
And landing in the mix of creatures, sand, and moonlight bath.

Focal Words: Pueo (A short-eared owl that is endemic to
Hawaii: poo-eh-o); Green ('ōma'oma'o: o-mah-o-mah-o)

Hula Girl

Focal Words: Teacher (kumu: koo-moo); A Polynesian form of dance (hula: who-lah); Red ('ula'ula: oo-luh-oo-luh)

The frayed ends of my grass skirt brushed up against my legs and I dropped my arm to itch the irritation. **Kumu** (koo-moo) had told us, "Remember: Smile big, girls!" **Hula** (who-lah) competitions made me nervous and I could never remember all the moves anyway, unlike Violet, who was always getting them right. I squinted my eyes against the stage lights to try to find my parents. Amidst the sea of "Aloha wear," flashing cameras, and parents oozing over their cute children, it was just impossible.

I mashed my pouted lips together and the **'ula'ula** (oo-luh-oo-luh) lipstick that was put on me now rested above my upper lip. When the music started, we all bowed our heads and pointed out toes towards the crowd. My head, however, was subtly turned to the right so that Violet was in my view just enough. When she stepped, I knew to step. When she spun, I knew to spin. Hula is more than just dance—it is the heartbeat of the Hawaiian people. It is the heartbeat of Violet. It is my heartbeat.

Focal Words: Teacher (kumu: koo-moo); A Polynesian form of dance (hula: who-lah); Red ('ula'ula: oo-luh-oo-luh)

Mauna Kea

Focal Words: Question (Nīele: nee-el-eh), Assemble ('Ākoakoa: ah-koh-ah-koah-ah), Pray (Pule: poo-leh)

The ocean labored to bare the world's tallest mountain. A place where gods dwell, where spirits reside. A place that snows on a tropical island. This is Mauna Kea! It is the tallest peak among all the islands. If we could **nīele** (nee-el-eh) our queen today, what would she want? Would she fight for this invaluable sacred space? Or, would she want us to launch into the 21st century? This is a topic of hot debate.

Hawaiians now fight for their land to keep this sacred space undeveloped. Others believe that its development will bring knowledge and prosperity to the islands and its inhabitants. Many people have gathered on Mauna Kea in peaceful protest. The Hawaiian people **'ākoakoa** (ah-koh-ah-koah-ah), dance, chant, and **pule** (poo-leh) that the development of this land be stopped. This stand is not only against future development, but past projects, too, which were promised not to take place. That was before money was involved. The government here is corrupt. Politicians would rather line their pockets with money than keep sacred lands untouched. We cannot and will never be able to move forward and innovate if we conveniently decorate over the places of the past.

Focal Words: Question (Nīele: nee-el-eh), Assemble ('Ākoakoa: ah-koh-ah-koah-ah), Pray (Pule: poo-leh)

COVID-19

Focal Words: Love (Aloha: ah-low-ha); Six ('Eono: ay-oh-no); Land ('Āina: ai-nuh)

Our small businesses have closed and, as the number of the infected rise, so does the number of the unemployed. Stay at home and isolate yourselves! **Aloha** (ah-low-ha) used to be spread through a hug or a kiss. Now these acts of love are acts that they say will endanger. We no longer greet each other with an affectionate embrace or a fond conversation. Put on a mask and stand **'eono** (ay-oh-no) feet away or else! But, as always, love finds her way. Aloha marches on. Aloha is spread through food distributions, volunteers, nurses, and janitors. Aloha was never lost; we just see her more clearly now in different acts. Love finds a way to live in the hearts and hands of the people of Hawai'i. Staying home heals the **'āina** (ai-nuh). Staying home lets the lungs of the ocean swell with clear blue waters. Staying home lets the turtles nest without worry upon empty beaches. Our land is thriving because of the break from constant tourism. Amid this pandemic, in this chaos, there is still healing.

Focal Words: Love (Aloha: ah-low-ha); Six ('Eono: ay-oh-no); Land ('Āina: ai-nuh)

Variation in Creation

Focal Words: Water (Wai: vai); Fire (Ahi: ah-he); Dwell (Noho: no-ho)

We have a lot of tropical showers on the island. **Wai** (vai) brings life and heals. It restores and replenishes, making our valleys lush, gardens green, and gives us a day to slow down. We also have **ahi** (ah-he) on this island. Lava is uncontrollably consumptive. But it is not chaotic. Chaos has no order and no purpose, but lava has a purpose—she is driven to make way for new life. She cleanses the ground by scorching the earth. And she erupts through the depth of the sea so that life may have a platform on which to **noho** (no-ho). Lava steams into the ocean like smoky lightning. The wai and ahi on this island have the same goal but work in distinct ways. Their differences are what allows life and variation in creation.

Focal Words: Water (Wai: vai); Fire (Ahi: ah-he); Dwell (Noho: no-ho)

Class of 2020

Focal Words: Fish (I'a: ee-uh); Pride (Ha'aheao: ha-ah-hay-oh); Congratulations (Ho'omaika'i: ho-oh-my-kah-ee)

Freshman year was a whole new ballgame in a whole new ballpark. We were now small **i'a** (ee-ah) in a big pond. We ranked last on the food chain and every grade above us knew it. Grades mattered now. And there were varsity tryouts along with new demanding schedules.

Sophomore year rolls around and we're feeling more confident. We're no longer one of those clueless freshmen. We walk with assurance, know more upper classman, and are ready to have fun this year.

Before you know it, we're juniors in high school. We're trying to cram in AP classes, get our licenses, maintain extracurricular activities, hold down jobs, and are always reminded that we have the start of college looming ahead of us. It's time to crack down. It's time to get serious, to make good relationships with teachers, and stay up all night studying.

Now we're seniors. It's the year of "lasts." Kings and Queens of the castle, we run this school. By now, I hope you have an answer to the favorite question: "Where are you going to college?" That's all any adult is going ask you. They may not realize, however, that you're worn out from high school and that you have sat staring at a blank document titled "College Essay" for weeks.

We're so close to the finish line that we just want to be put out of our misery. But, at the same time, we never want this moment to end. High school graduations in Hawai'i are a huge deal. Some parents watch their children receive the diploma that they were never handed. Some see their children become the first to attend college in their family. One should never underestimate the **ha'aheo** (ha-ah-hay-oh) and spirit that loved ones bring to a high school graduation in Hawai'i.

Graduates are showered with leis of flowers, food, money, and ribbons until their heads are buried. As a teenager, you will never make more money in two hours than at your graduation ceremony. Banners and signs of baby pictures and professional portraits are made to display school spirit. Multicolored leis stacked upon silk robes and the heartwarming fondness of high school memories are coming to an end. Still, graduation is a sign of hopefulness, excitement, and new adventure for the youth.

Four years of hard work (or the bare minimum) end tonight. This may be the end of a chapter filled with mistakes, SAT scores, hard work, AP tests, and friendships, but it is the beginning of a new story in life that you get to have control of. Most of us tried out best to be extraordinary students, athletes, volunteers, or musicians to make ourselves more appealing and desirable to colleges. We offered all our hard work and sacrifice to these institutions in hope of acceptance and validation. But remember what you've learned about yourself these last four years: You are enough. You don't need a panel of professors or the college board to tell you that.

No one could have predicted that the class of 2020 would be robbed of this extraordinary night of honor and celebration because of a global pandemic. The honor of shaking your headmaster's hand and receiving your diploma became, for this class, wishful thinking. Finishing high school with your best friends somehow, overnight, turned into separation via online classes. And that graduation party, well, it will have too many people and, as we all know, we have to follow social distancing rules. But…

To the class of 2020: We see all of your achievements. Your hard work was not and is not in vain. We love you. This whole island supports you. **Ho'omaika'i** (ho-oh-my-kah-ee)**!**

Focal Words: Fish (I'a: ee-uh); Pride (Ha'aheao: ha-ah-hay-oh); Congratulations (Ho'omaika'i: ho-oh-my-kah-ee)

Part III: Vocabulary Review

- A Polynesian form of dance (hula: who-lah)
- Assemble ('Ākoakoa: ah-koh-ah-koah-ah)
- Battles (Kaua: kah-oo-ah)
- Bless (Pōmaika'i: poh-my-kah-ee)
- Congratulations (Ho'omaika'i: ho-oh-my-kah-ee)
- Dwell (Noho: no-ho)
- Eyes (Maka: mah-kah)
- Feet (Wāwae: vah-vai)
- Fire (Ahi: ah-he)
- Fish (I'a: ee-uh)
- Green ('ōma'oma'o: o-mah-o-mah-o)
- Hands (Lima: lee-muh)
- Heart (Pu'uwai: poo-oo-vai)
- Land ('Āina: ai-nuh)
- Love (Aloha: ah-low-ha)
- Mouth (Waha: vah-ha)
- Peaceful Ocean (Kekaimalu: ke-kai-mah-loo)
- Pray (Pule: poo-leh)
- Pride (Ha'aheao: ha-ah-hay-oh)
- Pueo (A short-eared owl endemic to Hawaii: poo-eh-o)
- Question (Nīele: nee-el-eh)
- Rain (Ua: oo-ah)
- Red ('ula'ula: oo-luh-oo-luh)
- Six ('Eono: ay-oh-no)
- Strong Willed (Kamaehu: kah-mah-eh-hoo)
- Teacher (kumu: koo-moo)
- Thunder (Kahekili: kah-ha-key-lee)
- Voyage (Huaka'i: who-ah-kah-ee)
- Water (Wai: vai)
- Wind (Makani: mah-kuh-knee)

MAUI

House of the Sun

Focal Words: Mountain (Mauna: mau-nah); House of the sun (Haleakālā: ha-lei-ah-kah-lah); Honor (Hanohano: ha-no-ha-no)

 There stood two volcanos. A **mauna** (mau-nah) in the west, and a mauna in the east of the island. The mountain in the east is called **Haleakālā** (ha-lei-ah-kah-lah). This is a place where the sun himself was forced into submission in order to stretch the day's light. To **hanohano** (ha-no-ha-no) the covenant made that day, this mountain is named the house of the sun. The peak of Haleakālā sees 15 more minutes of the sun than the surrounding area.

Focal Words: Mountain (Mauna: mau-nah); House of the sun (Haleakālā: ha-lei-ah-kah-lah); Honor (Hanohano: ha-no-ha-no)

The Crutch of Hawai'i

Focal Words: Conflicted (Kū'ē: kooh-eeh); Ancient Hawaiian sacred site (Heiau: hey-au); Trash ('Opala: oh-pah-lah)

I feel **kū'ē** when I write these stories. I want you to know everything: the places, the people, the food, and the feeling. However, I don't want to put Hawai'i on a pedestal that attracts people so that they will come pollute her waters and buy her land. Yes, Hawai'i is a tropical island, but we face struggles of pollution, homelessness, and domestic violence just like any other state. People tend to see Hawai'i through the lens of a catalogue or brochure, which positions them so that they can easy overlook the imperfections of our land. The only way these islands stay as beguiling and enchanting as they are, is if negative human impact is kept at a minimum. People come to our islands for many reasons. It's the temporary visits, I believe, that have the most negative impact on the island. In a word: tourism. Tourism is like a crutch for our economy. We rely too heavily on the tourist industry here, especially for jobs. However, flying in and bussing around thousands of people every day causes rapid depletion of Hawaii's natural resources.

I have received a few messages from individuals who wanted to know how to come to Hawai'i and be respectful of the land and culture. When I read these messages, admittedly, I was overjoyed. Finally! People who look beyond their own desires in pursuit of doing the right thing! Having this attitude prior to arrival is amazing.

Please, take nothing from our islands but pictures. Especially do not take the rocks from a **heiau** (hey-au). These are believed to curse the owner until they are returned. Many people have disclosed their stories of misfortune after taking on of these pohaku until they returned them.

Please, waste nothing but time in these islands. Pick up your **'opala** (oh-pah-lah) at the beach and on hikes. Many people in our communities do organized beach walks to pick up 'opala. Bring a water bottle that you can refill it at your hotel so that you don't use plastic ones. Bring your own wooden utensils if you get takeout. Plastics and micro-plastics cover our shorelines and hurt our marine life. Do your part to contribute to the solution not the problem.

Please, leave nothing but your footprints in the sand.

Please, wear reef safe sunscreen so that the reefs have a chance to heal from the harmful properties of most sunscreens. On a busy tourist day, you can actually see the lining of oil from people's sunscreen on top of the water. Gross!

A struggle for many native Hawaiians is that they can no longer afford the land that their previous family might have owned. People with deep pockets who can afford such land buy it out and now the native Hawaiians have to live in government housing or Hawaiian homeland. This, of course, is not the reality in all cases. People who work hard for their money should be able to buy the land that they want. But land in Hawai'i is so expensive and the price is only expected to continue rising. Because of this, native Hawaiians whose ancestors lived and worked on the land cannot afford to stay in their own place of origin.

Whatever the solution to all these problems may be, they will not be instant or easy. The work in front of us is daunting and filled with corrupt politics. This is not to say either, that all tourism is bad; it does help our economy. But we locals need to ask ourselves a serious question and then answer it: At what point is the payout not worth the depletion of our island?

Focal Words: Conflicted (Kū'ē: kooh-eeh); Ancient Hawaiian sacred site (Heiau: hey-au); Trash ('Opala: oh-pah-lah)

Blood Quantum

Focal Words: A Pacific Islander (Kanaka: kah-nah-kah), Native (Maoli: mah-oh-lee) Group referring to hula (Hālau: ha-lau)

Being Hawaiian looks different on everyone. There are not certain features that a **kanaka** (kah-nah-kah) must have (or not have). Dark-skinned **maoli** (mah-oh-lee) or light skinned maoli are still kanaka! There is diversity among the Hawaiian people and it is beautiful. Within our line, we should not compare. Comparison kills. Especially "blood quantum" comparison. Asking someone "Eh how much Hawaiian are you?" may seem like a harmless question, when in reality that strategic inquiry stems from a place of violence. Having a greater percentage of Hawaiian ancestry in your blood doesn't make you "more" Hawaiian than someone who may have less.

Growing up in Hawaii, I've often felt like I never truly belonged. Although I have Hawaiian blood, I also have a "white" last name and lighter skin. I didn't belong to a **hālau** (ha-lau), and my family isn't fluent in the language. My mother has taught me about the culture, however, and the language that she knows. She taught me how to make leis and traditional foods. It took me 19 years to realize that being Hawaiian isn't merely distinguished through blood quantum, but actions. There is already so much division in the world, we do not need any within the Hawaiian race.

Focal Words: A Pacific Islander (Kanaka: kah-nah-kah), Native (Maoli: mah-oh-lee) Group referring to hula (Hālau: ha-lau)

Maui Mango

Focal Words: Gather (Hō'ili'ili: ho-ee-lee-ee-lee); Story (Mo'olelo: mo-oh-leh-lo); Summer (Kauwela: cow-veh-la)

All our family reunions take place on Maui. I have many cousins there and we all **hō'ili'ili** (ho-ee-lee-ee-lee) every other year to catch up, meet the new smallest members, and talk **mo'olelo** (mo-oh-leh-lo) about younger times and youthful days. My earliest memory from a family reunion is biting into a Maui mango. It was the color of the **kauwela** (cow-veh-la) sun and as sweet as the memories that we created there. The ripe golden juice stuck to my hands and cheeks, and the peels fell at my feet into the grass. I savored every bite and made sure to clean off the seed. My memories of family reunions bring me back to times as sweet as a Maui mango.

Focal Words: Gather (Hō'ili'ili: ho-ee-lee-ee-lee); Story (Mo'olelo: mo-oh-leh-lo); Summer (Kauwela: cow-veh-la)

Road to Hana

Focal Words: Waterfall (Lua Wai: loo-uh-vai); Happiness (Hau'oli: hauh-ooli); Misery (Pō'ino oki loa: poh-eenoh-okie-loah)

This winding road will take you back to where battles were fought, places where the gods left their marks. Along this journey, make sure to take your time. Everyone is in a rush. But you are on Hawaiian time! If you aren't looking out the window you could miss the **lua wai** (loo-uh-vai), beaches, and views that this island has to offer you. On a clear day, you might even be able to see Moloka'i on the horizon. When visiting the islands, remember that it's not all about the pictures. (Yes, it still happened if there's no photo!) We love to document our lives so much that, sometimes, we can forget to live them fully. Put down your camera and remember where you are. You are on the road to Hana! It's also as good a time and place as any to ask yourself where your own path in life is taking you? You are the author of your own **pō'ino oki loa** (poh-eenoh-okie-loah) and the author of your own **hau'loi** (hauh-ooli). Your road in life may be filled with obstacles that you have set there for yourself without realizing. On your drive here, take in this beautiful view and reflect it within yourself.

Focal Words: Waterfall (Lua Wai: loo-uh-vai); Happiness (Hau'oli: hauh-ooli); Misery (Pō'ino oki loa: poh-eenoh-okie-loah)

Drive-by Memories

Focal Words: To go for a stroll (Holoholo: ho-low-ho-low); Respect (Hō'ihi: ho-ee-hee); Move on (Hele: Heh-lay)

"Hey Nana, let's **holoholo**," I hollered. She liked going on drives through town. Her legs were starting to slow down and a drive was the perfect way to get her out of the house. She would always be taken aback by the newer and bigger buildings that replaced the previous. She was always stunned at how many houses were crammed together. She would tell me stories of growing up poor, playing outside 'til her father came home, and then jumping in the bushes to avoid his headlights. She remembered a particularly hot day from her childhood, one where she chewed the tar from the road as if it were gum. "Simpler times!" she called them.

I think there is a deep **hō'ihi** (ho-ee-hee) for the elderly in Hawai'i. This is not only because they babysat us at one point in our lives and nurtured us, but also because they made sacrifices and lived through hardships in order to give us, the new generation, a better shot at success. My Nana was working as a messenger girl on base when Pearl Harbor was bombed in 1941. For her, these are memories that seem like a lifetime ago but, to me, they are stories I love to hear and look forward to listening to.

"Let's **hele** home," I said. And we turned the car around and drove back.

Focal Words: To go for a stroll (Holoholo: ho-low-ho-low); Respect (Hō'ihi: ho-ee-hee); Move on (Hele: Heh-lay)

Underwater Kingdom

Focal Words: Salt (Pa'akai: pah-ah-kai); Older sister (Kaiku'ana: kai-koo-annah), Swim ('Au: ow)

We took the boat out early one morning before the waters grew crowded with other boaters. I sat on the edge of the vessel so I could feel the **pa'akai** (pah-ah-kai) spray graze my legs when the bow dipped down. I looked over to my **kaiku'ana** (kai-koo-annah) and said:

"Whoever can spot the most turtles wins!"
"Loser does the dishes!"
"Deal!" I smiled.

That day we spotted 16 turtles altogether. It was the most that I've ever seen in a day, even a month! On about the eighth turtle, we forgot about the score and were more amazed at just how many we were seeing. It was one thing to spot their glistening shells from above the water, but it was a whole other thing to **'au** (ow) next to them. Once I put my diving gear on and swam out to the reef, the turtles started coming up to me. They were extra curious that day and swam straight up to my face. I tried my best to keep my distance and not disturb them but, they were only more intrigued the more I backed away from them. One of the turtles was very old. He had hardened barnacles growing on his shell and a cataract in his left eye. Turtles were swimming about the waters, and some were tucked away beneath shelves of coral fast asleep. This was their home. And it was then that I understood that I was only a humble visitor in their underwater kingdom.

Focal Words: Salt (Pa'akai: pah-ah-kai); Older sister (Kaiku'ana: kai-koo-annah), Swim ('Au: ow)

Naya

Focal Words: Running (Holona: hoh-loh-nah); Empty (Hakahaka: ha-kah-ha-kah); Score (Helu: heh-looh)

A small girl, Naya clung to my back. I was breathing heavily, chasing after a soccer ball. She wrapped her arms tightly around my neck. The dust kicked up as more kids joined the game. Over my shoulder, I could see Naya's wild eyes full of excitement and happiness. Her smile was so big that she couldn't keep her mouth closed. Laughter overflowed from her on to me. The sun was setting behind one of the soccer posts and it casted a golden glow. I stopped **holona** (hoh-loh-nah) to catch my breath. Everything looked like a golden honey. Perfection!

Naya tugs at my hair and shouts that I need to keep running. But the boys **helu** (heh-looh) the final goal, and the game is over. The boys shout victoriously, flinging their hands above their heads while running victory laps. I laugh and crouch down so Naya can slip off my back.

"We'll win for sure next time," she said angrily. Her little nose scrunched up and her arms, as though they had a mind of their own, automatically crossed.

"Yes, we will!" I laughed. I grabbed her hand and started to walk her home.

Naya, along with the other kids playing with us, lived in low-income, government housing. Her home was located on the street between the Goodwill and the supermarket. The church was one street over. When we got to Naya's house, her expression changed. She let go of my hand and waved a faint goodbye. She walked into her one-room home where she lived with her parents, grandparents, and baby brother.

The games we play on Friday afternoons are what she looks forward to. She is free to laugh and run, but at home she sleeps on the floor so that her grandpa can have the bed.

One Friday, I returned to the field where we normally play. She didn't show. I waited until sunset and walked to her house to see if she was there. It was unusually quiet and their door was ajar. I pushed against the knob lightly and saw a dark, **hakahaka** (ha-kah-ha-kah) room. It was as if they had vanished.

It has been 5 years since I last saw her. I often wonder where she is today and why they left. Were they safe? A harrowing feeling comes upon me whenever I see her face in my mind.

Focal Words: Running (Holona: hoh-loh-nah); Empty (Hakahaka: ha-kah-ha-kah); Score (Helu: heh-looh)

Part IV: Vocabulary Review

- A Pacific Islander (Kanaka: kah-nah-kah)
- Ancient Hawaiian sacred site (Heiau: hey-au)
- Conflicted (Kū'ē: kooh-eeh)
- Empty (Hakahaka: ha-kah-ha-kah)
- Gather (Hō'ili'ili: ho-ee-lee-ee-lee)
- Group (referring to hula) (Hālau: ha-lau)
- Happiness (Hau'oli: hauh-ooli)
- Honor (Hanohano: ha-no-ha-no)
- House of the sun (Haleakālā: ha-lei-ah-kah-lah)
- Misery (Pō'ino oki loa: poh-eenoh-okie-loah)
- Mountain (Mauna: mau-nah)
- Move on (Hele: Heh-lay)
- Native (Maoli: mah-oh-lee)
- Older sister (Kaiku'ana: kai-koo-annah)
- Respect (Hō'ihi: ho-ee-hee)
- Running (Holona: hoh-loh-nah)
- Salt (Pa'akai: pah-ah-kai)
- Score (Helu: heh-looh)
- Story (Mo'olelo: mo-oh-leh-lo)
- Summer (Kauwela: cow-veh-la)
- Swim ('Au: ow)
- To go for a stroll (Holoholo: ho-low-ho-low)
- Trash ('Opala: oh-pah-lah)
- Waterfall (Lua Wai: loo-uh-vai)

KAUAI

Kalo Patch Kids

Focal Words: Mud   (Kelekele: keh-leh-keh-leh);   Ear
(Pepeiao: peh-peh-au); Dark (Maku'e: mah-koo-eh)

Before entering the kalo patch, we had to ask permission.
Uncle Dean and his family stood at the edge of the field and our
group anxiously lined up at the entrance like horses at the
starting gate. We all couldn't wait to get our hands dirty and
cool off in the mud. The chanting began. We sang to ask
permission to enter. And...he chanted back to grant us entrance.
And just like that, we were off. We ran down the hill in ragged
clothes, our feet beating against the side of the hill. Anything
that we were wearing today was bound to smell horrible and, if
you were really hard core at cleaning the kalo patch, you might
just have to throw away your clothes altogether. This was a kind
of labor that didn't feel like work.

We all split up to make our way weeding down separate
rows of the fields. We removed all the weeds, making sure to
get the roots, so that slippery mud was revealed in clusters and
the kalo wouldn't be choked out. The girls screamed when bugs
jumped out at them and the boys threw **kele-kele** (keh-leh-keh-
leh) at one another. Occasionally I would feel something
slippery rush past my leg. What was it?

At the end of the day we were beat. Our arms were sore
from weeding and hauling buckets of mud. Our legs were
covered in mud. And the sun had browned the back of our
necks. I pulled my body out of the mud and tried to scrape as
much as I could off my limbs. We lined up at the hose and
washed off what we could of the day's work. Mud remained in
our **pepeiao** (peh-peh-au) and in our toes. There was no way we
would be getting this horrible smell off us by tomorrow. We

decided to wash off in the ocean. We all ran from the sand and let the water catch us. Instantly, the water around us turned **maku'e** (mah-koo-eh) as we scrubbed and wrung out our clothes.

Focal Words: Mud   (Kelekele: keh-leh-keh-leh);   Ear (Pepeiao: peh-peh-au); Dark (Maku'e: mah-koo-eh)

The Birthday You Won't Remember

Focal Words: Celebration (Ho'olaule'a: ho-oh-lau-leh-ah); Birthday (Lā hānau: lah-ha-nau); Sleep (Hiamoe: he-ah-moh-eeh)

For local families, a child's first birthday is a big **ho'olaule'a** (ho-oh-lau-leh-ah). For my first **lā hānau** (lah-ha-nau), my mother rented out an entire restaurant and invited all our family members and friends to fill the tables. There were balloons and music but, by the time it got to the cake, I had passed out in my stroller seat. So, why make such a big deal out of something that the baby won't even remember?

Back in the early days of Hawai'i, it was a joyous occasion for a baby to live past infancy. After one year of no fatal sicknesses or accidents, the child's life was celebrated by all. That is why a baby's first birthday is a big celebration here. I've looked at photographs from that night. All my relatives that I know now look so young and happy. My uncle has a full set of hair in these pictures! Everyone was unknowingly living in their "good old days," while my days had just begun. My mom dressed me in a teal Chinese wrap dress. I had jade bracelets on my baby cherub arms and, before the cake was served, I discovered **hiamoe** (he-ah-moh-eeh) in my stroller.

Focal Words: Celebration (Ho'olaule'a: ho-oh-lau-leh-ah); Birthday (Lā hānau: lah-ha-nau); Sleep (Hiamoe: he-ah-moh-eeh)

The Dating Game

Focal Words: Today   (Kēia lā: keh-ee-ah-lah); Blood (Koko: koh-koh); Strong (Ikaika: ee-kaih-kah)

Hawai'i is filled with a variety of ethnicities. There are people here from all around the world. We are a diverse melting pot in the middle of the Pacific Ocean. It is more common than not to see people who are "mixed race." Back when Hawai'i relied on farming rather than tourism, our coffee, sugarcane, and pineapple industry kept us going. But farming is hard work, and the businessman who were running these plantations, wanted to pay for cheaper labor. Many men came from China to find work in our sugar cane fields. Some of them returned to China or sent the money to their families there. Others started families with the local women here.

Kēia lā there is much more diversity, however, there is more than merely Hawaiian and Chinese **koko** (koh-koh). Yet, it is these two cultures that have influenced our family values. This is a good thing. But, if you were born and raised here, one day you may come to find out that you are related or a distant cousin of one of your friends! This is a good thing, too. But there is a downside: When you are planning to date someone you always need to know who their aunties, uncles, and grandparents are. You don't want to end up dating a relative! Yes, our family values are **ikaika** (ee-kaih-kah), but not like *that*!

Focal Words: Today (Kēia l: ākeh-ee-ah-lah); Blood (Koko: koh-koh); Strong (Ikaika: ee-kaih-kah)

Worship

Focal Words: Lungs (Akemāmā: ah-keh-mah-mah); Rainbow (Anuenue: ah-noo-eh-noo-eh), Church (Hale pule: ha-lei poo-lei)

I stood under a waterfall so large that the crashing sound in my ears was deafening and the force of the pounding water against my back took the air out of my **akemāmā** (ah-keh-mah-mah). All my senses were numbed and heightened to the waterfall's heartbeat. The sun surrounded the mist the fall gave off, and an **anuenue (ah-noo-eh-noo-eh)** formed in the center of the waters and outstretched into the sky. This is my form of worship. A **hale pule** (ha-lei poo-lei) filled of holy water from the falls, the glory of the Lord in the sun, and his promise to us in an anuenue.

Focal Words: Lungs (Akemāmā: ah-keh-mah-mah); Rainbow (Anuenue: ah-noo-eh-noo-eh), Church (Hale pule: ha-lei poo-lei)

70

The Hawai'i Do's and Don'ts

Focal Words: A (white) person who is not native Hawaiian (Haole: how-leeh), Wave (Nalu: nah-loo); Steal ('Aihue au: aye-hoo-eh-au)

If you've never been to Hawai'i before, I suggest that you do your research before coming. Don't just look up the top 10 best beaches and bars. Don't look just look up the rent a car places and hotel accommodations. Do your research on our culture, on the language, on our history. This trip will be more enjoyable for you if you do these things. Ignorance is not bliss here. That isn't to say that every **haole (how-leeh)** from the mainland is ignorant, but you would be surprised at how many people who come here for a "vacation" are. The term haole can literally be translated as "one without breath." This means that you are not Native Hawaiian or local. The biggest thing locals are looking for here is respect. The Hawaiian people have had a lot taken away from them and have endured much suffering. This is not to victimize us, but simply to inform you that associations with past indiscretions are often traced back to haoles.

For example, if you are in the water trying to catch a **nalu** (nah-loo) and there is an entire line up of local surfers, do not try to cut them off or **'aihue** (aye-hoo-eh-au) a nalu. It seems like common knowledge and surfer etiquette, but this is one of the ways that ignorance from mainlanders comes into play a lot!

The next thing to know has to do with driving. If you rent a fancy or flashy car, it's easy to narrow down that you are either a tourist or from the military. Don't try to take up two parking spaces so that your car doesn't get scratched; if anything, this makes it a prime target. If you are going on a hike or traversing beach access located in a residential community, do not block the homeowner's driveway or mailbox! Be respectful and park a little ways down the street and walk. While driving, if another car lets you in a lane or gives you the go ahead, it's standard courtesy to throw them a shaka or wave. This is one that a lot of people forget, but showing this little act of gratitude is much appreciated!

One of the most important rules when visiting our island is to pick up your trash. Don't leave that wrapper or water bottle on the beach or in the bushes. You can't just show the people here respect, you need to show the island respect, too.

The final rule, and one that makes me the most upset, has to do with people showing no respect to our aquatic life here and ignoring boundaries. It disgusts and saddens me to see tourists willing to do anything for a photo or video, even if that means intruding the space of endangered species. You can go without that cool selfie; I'm sure you've taken a hundred more elsewhere.

Hawaiian monk seals are endangered animals and will often lay in the sand to take a nap. Usually, there will be a perimeter up around them so that people know not to approach. If you come across one who hasn't been spotted by marine safety yet, well, keep your distance. Not only are these animals endangered, they are dangerous. Further, while you're in the water, it can be cool to have a turtle swim up to you. If this happens, make sure not to touch them. Also, do not chase after them. You are visitors in their home.

All these rules should seem like common knowledge. They embody common courtesy and show cultural respect. But, for some reason, tourists are prone to breaking these rules. Once again, I would like to reiterate that associations with past indiscretions are often traced back to haoles. That is why I continue to stress respect so much when visiting the islands. I want your vacation to be more enjoyable and I do not want you to run into problems with the locals here. Remember: You want to leave this land better than you found it.

Focal Words: A (white) person who is not native Hawaiian (Haole: how-leeh), Wave (Nalu: nah-loo); Steal ('Aihue au: aye-hoo-eh-au)

Ono Grindz

Focal Words: Delicious (Ono: oh-noh), Staple Hawaiian food from taro plant (Poi: poy); Raw fish cut into chunks (Poke: poh-keh)

Returning from my freshman year at a mainland collage, I could not wait to arrive at home! Of course, I had a great time, and it was full of new experiences, but I missed the taste of local food. If you were born and raised in Hawai'i, your first food was probably poi (poy). **Poi** is a thick taro paste that is **ono (oh-noh)** with lau lau or rice.

On a hot sunny day, however, all I want to eat is an ice cold rainbow shave ice. The sweet syrup is refreshing and so ono. Another island favorite is a musubi. I take a traditional twist on mine and go for a teriyaki tofu musubi. But if you're old school, you probably want the spam version.

We love our rice here. We eat it for breakfast, lunch, and dinner. Rice is a staple for every meal. It was the first thing that I learned to make in the kitchen. On the days that my mom had work, I would always make sure to start the pot of rice so that it would be fresh when she got home.

Having access to fresh fruit every day is something I took for granted before I went to college. If you're lucky, your house might have a coconut, papaya, mango, or lychee tree! And if you're a friendly neighbor to one of these houses, you bet that when that fruit is in season, you will be sharing the harvest. And if you're not a friendly neighbor? Well, you might get lucky and have a coconut drop into your yard every once in a while.

Of course, living so close to the ocean, seafood is prime. My father built his boat with his own two hands and with the love and pride of a fisherman. He would be up at 3 in the morning and out until 10 at night working. He wanted to be out on the water early and, after a full day of work, he would go to the fish markets to sell his catch of the day. He spent more time on the water than he did on the land. Another local favorite, of the seafood sort, is the **poke (poh-keh)** bowl. You can get it spicy or salty. The fresher the better! The flavors of these islands are something that simply cannot be found all in one place anywhere else.

Focal Words: Delicious (Ono: oh-noh), Staple Hawaiian food from taro plant (Poi: poy); Raw fish cut into chunks (Poke: poh-keh)

Aunty and Uncle

Focal Words: Talk (Wala'au: vah-lah-ow), Related (Pee-lee); Single (Ho'okahi: ho-oh-kah-ee)

My love of language is part of the reason why this book is written the way it is. I think that language dropping (like the way each chapter is written) has a certain beauty that can enhance the meaning and practice of the language being dropped. In this case, the focus is Hawaiian. The way language is used in Hawai'i is very important because, it is through songs and stories, that our traditions were passed on throughout the generations. When we engage in **wala'au** (vah-lah-ow) with each other, the language is relaxed and casual. We address our elders with "Aunty" and "Uncle." We don't have to be **pili** (pee-lee) in the slightest, but this creates a sense of family. This is what we call our parent's friends, our friend's parents, and so on.

Another part of the way we speak to each other can be in Hawaiian Pidgin. If I had to describe what Pidgin sounds like to someone who has never heard it, I would say that is a shortened way of speaking that focuses on **ho'okahi** (ho-oh-kah-ee) syllables. I think there is a time and a place to speak Pidgin. For example, I would not use it if I was in a job interview or writing any kind of letter. I would use it if I was casually talking to my parents, or friends. Here are some samples.

Example 1:
English: What restaurant do you want to eat at?
Pidgin: Where you like eat?

Example 2:
English: Goodbye, have a good day!
Pidgin: Shoots den brah. Have a good one.

Through these examples, you can see the differences and are able to identify the stress on single syllables in pidgin. Alright, shoots den!

Focal Words: Talk (Wala'au: vah-lah-ow), Related (pee-lee); Single (Ho'okahi: ho-oh-kah-ee)

My Hawai'i

Focal Words: The life of the land is perpetuated in righteousness (Ua Mau ke Ea o ka 'Āina i ka pono: oo-ah mau keh eh-ah oh kah ai-nah ee kah pono)

No matter where I go in life, I know that Hawai'i will always be waiting for me. When I am away, I can feel it's pull like the ebb of the ocean's tide. I dream of going back to her warm tropical breeze and feeling her sand beneath my feet. There is something about Hawai'i that is indescribable. If you were born and raised here, you know what I mean. Local knowledge is paramount in these islands. Indeed, Hawai'i just has a thing about her that is so intoxicating and special that, if you live here, it bonds you to this island for life. This book is full of my stories and the experiences Hawai'i has given to me. I am forever grateful for these life lessons and memories. Ua Mau ke Ea o ka 'Āina i ka pono.

Focal Words: The life of the land is perpetuated in righteousness (Ua Mau ke Ea o ka 'Āina i ka pono: oo-ah mau keh eh-ah oh kah ai-nah ee kah pono)

Part V: Vocabulary Review

- A (white) person who is not native Hawaiian (Haole: how-leeh)
- Birthday (Lā hānau: lah-ha-nau)
- Blood (Koko: koh-koh)
- Celebration (Ho'olaule'a: ho-oh-lau-leh-ah)
- Church (Hale pule: ha-lei poo-lei)
- Dark (Maku'e: mah-koo-eh)
- Delicious (Ono: oh-noh)
- Ear (Pepeiao: peh-peh-au)
- Lungs (Akemāmā: ah-keh-mah-mah)
- Mud (Kelekele: keh-leh-keh-leh)
- Rainbow (Anuenue: ah-noo-eh-noo-eh)
- Raw fish cut into chunks (Poke: poh-keh)
- Related (Pee-lee)
- Single (Ho'okahi: ho-oh-kah-ee)
- Sleep (Hiamoe: he-ah-moh-eeh)
- Staple Hawaiian food from taro plant (Poi: poy)
- Steal ('Aihue au: aye-hoo-eh-au)
- Strong (Ikaika: ee-kaih-kah)
- Talk (Wala'au: vah-lah-ow)
- The life of the land is perpetuated in righteousness (Ua Mau ke Ea o ka 'Āina i ka pono: oo-ah mau keh eh-ah oh kah ai-nah ee kah pono)
- Today (Kēia lā: keh-ee-ah-lah)
- Wave (Nalu: nah-loo)

Glossary

- A (white) person who is not native Hawaiian (Haole: how-leeh)
- A Pacific Islander (Kanaka: kah-nah-kah)
- A Polynesian form of dance (hula: who-lah)
- A type of ray-finned fish found in tropical waters (Mahi Mahi: mah-he-mah-he)
- Ahuimanu - A street name in the district of Kaneohe, which can literally mean "Flock of birds" (Ahuimanu: ah-hoo-ie-mah-new)
- Ancient Hawaiian sacred site (Heiau: hey-au)
- Assemble ('Ākoakoa: ah-koh-ah-koah-ah)
- Baby (Pēpē: peh-peh)
- Battles (Kaua: kah-oo-ah)
- Beach (Kahakai: ka-ha-kai)
- Bird (Manu: mah-noo)
- Birthday (Lā hānau: lah-ha-nau)
- Black ('Ele'ele: eh-lay-eh-lay)
- Bless (Pōmaika'i: poh-my-kah-ee)
- Blood (Koko: koh-koh)
- Blue (Polū: po-loo)
- Boat (Moku: mo-koo)
- Breadfruit (Ulu: oo-loo)
- Broken (Poloke: poh-loh-keh)
- Brown (Ehu: eh-who)
- Celebration (Ho'olaule'a: ho-oh-lau-leh-ah)
- Chicken (Moa: moh-ah)
- Chief (Ali'i: ah-lee-ee)
- Children (Keiki: kay-kee)
- Church (Hale pule: ha-lei poo-lei)

- Colors (Waiho'olu'u: vai-ho-oh-loo-oo)
- Conflicted (Kū'ē: kooh-eeh)
- Congratulations (Ho'omaika'i: ho-oh-my-kah-ee)
- Crowd (Lehulehu: leh-who-leh-who) Crazy (Lōlō: loh-loh)
- Dark (Maku'e: mah-koo-eh)
- Delicious (Ono: oh-noh)
- Dwell (Noho: no-ho)
- Ear (Pepeiao: peh-peh-au)
- Elders (Kapuna: kah-poo-nah)
- Empty (Hakahaka: ha-kah-ha-kah)
- Eyes (Maka: mah-kah)
- Eyes (Maka: mah-kah)
- Family (Ohana: oh-ha-nah)
- Father (Makuakane: mah-koo-ah-kah-nay)
- Feet (Wāwae: vah-vai)
- Finished (Pau: pow)
- Fire (Ahi: ah-he)
- Fish (I'a: ee-uh)
- Fish on (Hanapa'a: ha-nah-pah-ah)
- Fishpond (Loko'ia: loco-ee-ah)
- Friends (Hoaloha: ho-ah-loh-ha)
- Fruit (Hua: hoo-ah)
- Gather (Hō'ili'ili: ho-ee-lee-ee-lee)
- Goddess of fire and volcanoes (Pele: peh-lay)
- Grandmother (Kapuna Wahine: kah-poo-nah-wah-he-nay)
- Green ('ōma'oma'o: o-mah-o-mah-o)
- Group (referring to hula) (Hālau: ha-lau)
- Hair (Lauoho: lau-oh-ho)
- Half (Hapa: hah-pah)
- Hands (Lima: lee-muh)

- Happiness (Hau'oli: hauh-ooli)
- Harmony (Lokahi: low-kah-he)
- Heart (Pu'uwai: poo-oo-vai)
- Heleconia - A tropical vibrant hanging plant (Heleconia: hel-leh-cone-yah)
- Help (Kokua: koh-koo-ah)
- Holes (Puka: poo-kah)
- Honor (Hanohano: ha-no-ha-no)
- House (Hale: ha-lay)
- House of the sun (Haleakālā: ha-lei-ah-kah-lah)
- Island (Moku: moh-koo)
- Ka'a'awa - A city on the far east side of O'ahu (Ka'a'awa: kah-ah-ah-vuh)
- Kailua - A town on the east side on O'ahu (Kailua: kai-loo-ah)
- Kane'ohe - A city on the east side of O'ahu (Kane'ohe: kah-nay-oh-hay)
- Land ('Āina: ai-nuh)
- Leaves of the hala tree (Lauhala: lau-ha-la)
- Loincloth (Malo: mah-low)
- Love (Aloha: ah-low-ha)
- Lungs (Akemāmā: ah-keh-mah-mah)
- Man (Kāne: kah-nay)
- Misery (Pō'ino oki loa: poh-eenoh-okie-loah)
- Morning (Kakahiaka: kah-kah-he-akah)
- Mother (Makuawahine: mah-koo-ah-wah-he-nay)
- Mountain (Mauna: mau-nah)
- Mouth (Waha: vah-ha)
- Move on (Hele: Heh-lay)
- Mud (Kelekele: keh-leh-keh-leh)
- Native (Maoli: mah-oh-lee)
- Night (Pō: po)

- Ocean (Moana: moh-ah-nah)
- Older sister (Kaikuʻana: kai-koo-annah)
- Peaceful Ocean (Kekaimalu: ke-kai-mah-loo)
- Pray (Pule: poo-leh)
- Pride (Haʻaheao: ha-ah-hay-oh)
- Pueo (A short-eared owl that is endemic to Hawaii: poo-eh-o)
- Question (Nīele: nee-el-eh)
- Rain (Ua: oo-ah)
- Rainbow (Anuenue: ah-noo-eh-noo-eh)
- Raw fish cut into chunks (Poke: poh-keh)
- Red (ʻulaʻula: oo-luh-oo-luh)
- Related (Pee-lee)
- Respect (Hōʻihi: ho-ee-hee)
- Rock (pōhaku: poh-ha-koo)
- Running (Holona: hoh-loh-nah)
- Salt (Paʻakai: pah-ah-kai)
- Sand (One: oh-ney)
- Score (Helu: heh-looh)
- Sea (Kai: kuy)
- Sing (Mele: meh-lay)
- Single (Hoʻokahi: ho-oh-kah-ee)
- Six (ʻEono: ay-oh-no)
- Sky (Wākea: wah-keh-ah)
- Sleep (Hiamoe: he-ah-moh-eeh)
- Spiritual energy of power and strength (Mana: muh-nuh)
- Staple Hawaiian food from taro plant (Poi: poy)
- Star (Hoku: ho-koo)
- Steal (ʻAihue au: aye-hoo-eh-au)
- Story (Moʻolelo: mo-oh-leh-lo)
- Strong (Ikaika: ee-kaih-kah)

- Strong willed (Kamaehu: ka-mah-eh-who)
- Strong Willed (Kamaehu: kah-mah-eh-hoo)
- Summer (Kauwela: cow-veh-la)
- Sun (La: lah) Clouds (Ao: ow)
- Swim ('Au: ow)
- Talk (Wala'au: vah-lah-ow)
- Teacher (kumu: koo-moo)
- Thank you (Mahalo: mah-ha-low)
- The life of the land is perpetuated in righteousness (Ua Mau ke Ea o ka 'Āina i ka pono: oo-ah mau keh eh-ah oh kah ai-nah ee kah pono)
- Thunder (Kahekili: kah-ha-key-lee)
- To go for a stroll (Holoholo: ho-low-ho-low)
- Today (Kēia lā: keh-ee-ah-lah)
- Trash ('Opala: oh-pah-lah)
- Until we meet again (A hui ho: ah-who-ee-hoh)
- Volcano (Luapele: loo-uh-pay-lay)
- Voyage (Huaka'i: who-ah-kah-ee)
- Waikiki - A resort area in Honolulu (Waikiki: why-kee-kee)
- Water (Wai: vai)
- Waterfall (Lua Wai: loo-uh-vai)
- Wave (Nalu: nah-loo)
- Wind (Makani: mah-kuh-knee)
- Women (Wahine: wah-he-nay)
- Work (Hana: hah-nah)
- Young (Ōpio: oh-pee-oh)

NOTES

NOTES

NOTES

NOTES

NOTES

NOTES

www.ingramcontent.com/pod-product-compliance
Lightning Source LLC
Chambersburg PA
CBHW070055100426
42740CB00013B/2848